I Kissed Dating
GOODBYE
STUDY GUIDE

JOSHUA HARRIS

WITH SHANNON HARRIS AND NICOLE WHITACRE

Multnomah® Publishers

I KISSED DATING GOODBYE STUDY GUIDE
published by Multnomah Publishers
A division of Random House, Inc.

© 1999, 2003 by Joshua Harris
International Standard Book Number: 1-59052-136-6
Original ISBN: 1-57673-652-0

Cover design by The Office of Bill Chiaravalle
Cover image by Getty Images / Stephanie Rausser

Unless otherwise indicated, Scripture quotations are from:
The Holy Bible, New International Version
© 1973, 1984 by International Bible Society,
used by permission of Zondervan Publishing House
Also quoted:
The Message © 1993 by Eugene H. Peterson
The Holy Bible, New King James Version (NKJV) ©1979,
1982 by Thomas Nelson, Inc.

Multnomah is a trademark of Multnomah Publishers
and is registered in the U.S. Patent and Trademark Office.
The colophon is a trademark of Multnomah Publishers.

Printed in the United States of America.

For information:
Multnomah Publishers
12265 Oracle Boulevard, Suite 200
Colorado Springs, CO 80921

06 07 08 09 10—13 12 11 10 9

To C. J. and Carolyn Mahaney

Contents

How to Use This Study Guide

THE *I KISSED DATING GOODBYE STUDY GUIDE* was created to help people share in the journey of seeking God's will for romance. It's designed to spark dialogue and get people talking openly and honestly about relationships. Most important, it challenges participants to apply the principles of *I Kissed Dating Goodbye* (IKDG) to their lives.

WHO CAN USE IT?

The *IKDG Study Guide* is extremely versatile. It can be used by a group or by an individual, who answers the questions in a private journal.

The study guide is written primarily for two or more people who want to walk through the book together. Whether this is a group of five friends who meet weekly at a coffee shop or twenty people in a Sunday school class, this guide can be adapted to meet your needs.

HOW TO LEAD A GROUP

Regardless of the size of the group, it's helpful to have one person serve as the leader. This person assigns the appropriate chapter for the group to read before the meeting, leads in asking the questions, and facilitates discussion.

If you're the one leading, you'll find that the study guide is designed to make your job as easy as possible. Following is a description of the elements included in each chapter and how they can serve you.

CHAPTER AT A GLANCE

This summary is a great way to quickly familiarize yourself with the essence of each chapter from the book. It's also written to be read out loud to your group to refresh their memory. (A "Key Quote" and "Key Scripture" is included along with a list of Scripture passages referenced in the chapter.)

GOAL OF DISCUSSION

The "Goal of Discussion" gives you a succinct game plan for you and your group to focus on. It can also be read aloud to your group.

QUESTIONS

Ten questions are included for each chapter. They're divided into categories that allow you to start off on a lighter note and then ease into more serious questions.

Icebreakers

These discussion starters are nonthreatening ways to get people talking. Have fun with these.

Getting Serious

These midrange questions ask what people think of ideas or concepts in the book. They're more intellectually provoking than the *Icebreakers* but less personal than the *Being Real* questions that follow.

Being Real

These are the most important questions because they point to application. They take the discussion from "What do you think about an idea?" to "How are you living your life, and what are you going to do to change?" Try to spend most of your time on these questions.

Just for Guys and Just for Girls

Here you'll find one question for guys and one for girls. This is helpful if you're meeting with a group of the same sex or if you separate a mixed group toward the end of a meeting.

REFLECTION

Each chapter closes with a brief personal commentary on the chapter by the author. Joshua then expands on the chapter topic, clarifies a point, or just takes things in an unexpected direction. Group leaders will find it helpful to read the "Reflection" before leading a meeting and in some cases to read it aloud to the group to spark discussion.

MORE TIPS FOR LEADING A GROUP

I. STRIVE FOR APPLICATION

James 1:22 says, "Do not merely listen to the word, and so deceive your-selves. Do what it says." Remind the people in your group that merely reading a book and talking about it won't produce change. Real change occurs after we close the book and do something about it. As you progress through the study guide, take time during your meetings to have people share what changes they've made.

2. START SMALL

While application is important, no one can change in every area all at once. Encourage members of your group to begin by trying to apply just *one* point from the chapter.

3. OUTLAW ONE-WORD ANSWERS

The questions in the *IKDG Study Guide* were written to provoke discussion and even debate. Ban yes and no answers. Encourage people in your group to share from their hearts, not just parrot the "right" answer from *I Kissed Dating Goodbye*. Giving only expected or "acceptable" answers will not help them examine their own lives.

4. LISTEN TO THE HOLY SPIRIT

This study guide exists to serve *you*—don't become a slave to it. If one question opens up a fruitful discussion, go with it! Don't feel you have to work through all of the questions. Take opportunities for the group to pray spontaneously for someone who expresses a need. Let God's Spirit, not this book's format, guide you.

5. Encourage, Encourage, Encourage!

Make sure to tell people when you see them growing in a certain area—no matter how small it is. The best way to motivate your group members is to offer lots of praise and encouragement.

6. Focus on God

In the midst of focusing on human relationships, make sure that the group's primary motive is to please and honor God. Begin and end your time with prayer.

Enjoy the journey! Remember, only God's Spirit can work real change in our lives. May your group's use of this study guide be used by God to bring about life-changing results.

NEW FEATURE: STUDY QUESTIONS FOR THE I KISSED DATING GOODBYE VIDEO SERIES

We have also included study questions to accompany the I Kissed Dating Goodbye Video Series created by Josh Harris and Multnomah Publishers (this series was previously titled Searching for True Love). The series consists of three videos (*Love, Purity,* and *Trust*) that further explore some of the topics discussed in *I Kissed Dating Goodbye*. These videos are an ideal companion to this study guide. Mixing drama, real-life testimonials, and on-the-street interviews with challenging messages from Josh, the videos are fast-paced and engaging. They're perfect for any-size group (such as a Sunday school class, youth group, or even a small group meeting in a living room) to encourage discussion and growth.

So This Is Love?

Beyond What Feels Good, Back to What *Is* Good

CHAPTER AT A GLANCE

Chapter 1 opens with the story of Anna's wedding nightmare. It illustrates how typical dating cheats us and our future spouse out of all that God intends for us in marriage. Each girlfriend or boyfriend we have takes a piece of our heart when the relationship ends.

If we want God's best in our relationships, we have to play by His rules. Instead of following the world's patterns of dating, we must take our cues from His Word and learn biblical or "smart" love (Philippians 1:9–10). The priority of this kind of love is not our needs, our selfish desires, or even our feelings, but pleasing God and doing what is best for others. If we are willing to break away from the harmful patterns of typical dating, we can discover God's best for our lives.

KEY QUOTE

"God's lordship in my life doesn't merely tinker with my approach to romance—it completely transforms it. God not only wants me to act differently; He wants me to *think* differently—to view love, purity, and singleness from His perspective, to have a new lifestyle and a new attitude."

KEY SCRIPTURE

Philippians 1:9–10: "And this is my prayer: that your love may abound more and more in knowledge and depth of insight, so that you may be able to discern what is best and may be pure and blameless until the day of Christ." (Also see Matthew 10:29 and Luke 12:2.)

THE GOAL OF DISCUSSION

The goal for our first discussion is to evaluate whether or not our relationships with the opposite sex are based on a biblical definition of love and purity. If they aren't, what areas need to change in our hearts and lifestyles?

ICEBREAKERS

1. What was your response when you first heard about *I Kissed Dating Goodbye*? How would you rate your response on a scale from one to ten (one being "Oh, yuck!" and ten being "Sounds great!")? Why?
2. In the introduction (page 9), Josh says that *IKDG* isn't about how to make dating work for you, but how to make your life pleasing to God. Are you interested in exploring this idea?

GETTING SERIOUS

1. In what ways are we tempted to accept our culture's idea of romance instead of the Bible's?
2. According to Josh, why are short-term dating relationships harmful? Do you agree that there is something better? Why or why not?

BEING REAL

1. Describe your reaction to Anna's dream (pages 13–4). How does thinking about your wedding day motivate you to make changes in the way you relate to the opposite sex right now?
2. Read Philippians 1:9–10. If you desire something better in relationships, how does this verse challenge your perspective on love?
3. What's one way you can show sincere and intelligent love in your relationships?
4. Josh writes, "The God who sees all our sin is ready to forgive if we repent and turn from it. He calls us to a new way of life." Are there sins from past relationships you need to turn from and receive forgiveness for? If so, what would hinder you from doing that right now?

JUST FOR GUYS

If God's best for our lives includes treating girls as sisters in Christ rather than as potential girlfriends, what does that mean practically?

JUST FOR GIRLS

Let's face it, when it comes to feeling driven love, girls are the experts. How can we avoid being led by our feelings or emotions in relationships?

REFLECTION

The one thing that usually stands out to people in chapter 1 is Anna's wedding nightmare. Several people have told me they broke down crying when they read it. Many were made aware for the first time of the harmful and long-lasting consequences of their past relationships.

But at times I've wondered if the dream was too strong, too effective at reminding people of their mistakes without offering redemption. Would they feel hopeless and believe that their chance for a happy marriage was ruined?

I did my best to make sure that wasn't their experience. Throughout the book, I pointed to the hope and forgiveness God offers through the death and resurrection of Jesus. No matter how many former boyfriends or girlfriends we've had or how much we've sinned, God will forgive us and give us the grace we need to live obedient lives through faith in Christ. That's the good news of the gospel.

But that's not all the Bible tells us. It's also replete with warnings about the danger of sin. As Romans 6:23 says, "For the wages of sin is death, but the gift of God is eternal life in Christ Jesus our Lord." In this one verse we're given both warning and hope.

I wanted to give both in I Kissed Dating Goodbye. That's why I started with something as stark and nightmarish as Anna's dream. The wages of sin *are* stark and nightmarish, and I wanted to grab people's attention and awaken them to the reality of sin's awful consequences.

I've received thousands of letters from people of every age who wish they'd been awakened earlier in life. One girl, a freshman in college, wrote me this letter:

When I was a little girl, my parents made it very clear that they were against dating. However, when I turned sixteen, I decided that I was old enough to make my own decisions regarding relationships. I believed that dating was my teenage right.

If I had only known that a few years later I would regret not listening and obeying what my parents said. If I had known all the hurt dating would cause me, I never would have done it. The pain is now unbearable.

It has been over a year since I broke up with my boyfriend. I have done everything possible to erase his memory from my heart. My parents helped me burn the hundreds of love letters he had given to me through the years. I threw away all of the birthday presents and Christmas presents. I took down all of the pictures of him. But I haven't forgotten him.

I now attend a Christian college thousands of miles away from my old boyfriend, and I've dated many different guys. I thought a new boyfriend would make me forget him; and when my old boyfriend called me at college, I didn't return his phone call. When he e-mailed me, I erased his address from my computer and refused to write him back. I did absolutely everything to try to forget, but I still remember.

This girl now understands that giving your heart to someone is serious. It's not as easy to walk away from an intimate relationship as some think.

You might relate to her story. Maybe you have regrets and are now doing your best to live for God. Don't lose hope. God's grace is sufficient to cover your sin and help you move on. But there are others who are still wavering. Obedience to God looks boring—pursuing the world and its pleasure appears tantalizing. Please take the warning from this chapter to heart. May it shock you and sober you—and in doing so lead you to life.

◦◦◦

The Little Relationship Principle

(That Leads to Big Change)

The Joy of Intimacy Is the Reward of Commitment

CHAPTER AT A GLANCE

In this chapter Josh shares what he calls the Little Relationship Principle:

The joy of intimacy is the reward of commitment.

He tells the story about his appearance on the TV show *Politically Incorrect* and his attempt to explain why there's something better than merely being "out for a good time" in relationships. He examines the history of dating to show that its main problem is that it encourages people to selfishly disconnect the pursuit of romance from the pursuit of commitment. He shows why God wants us to reconnect the two and the wonderful change that takes place in our relationships when we do.

KEY QUOTE

An intimate relationship is a beautiful experience that God wants us to enjoy. After all, He stated that it wasn't good for man to be alone and created the woman to perfectly complement him and help him (Genesis 2:18). But God has made the fulfillment of intimacy a by-product of commitment-based love. If we want to experience the goodness of His plan, we need to reconnect the pursuit of intimacy with the pursuit of commitment.

KEY SCRIPTURE

Proverbs 3:3: "Let love and faithfulness never leave you; bind them around your neck, write them on the tablet of your heart." (See also 1 Thessalonians 4:6; 1 Timothy 5:1–2; and Matthew 22:39.)

GOAL OF DISCUSSION

The purpose of this chapter is to discover God's special gift of intimacy and romance for us—which comes through the important step of commitment. We will discuss how this perspective on dating relationships has been lost in current society and how to reclaim it.

ICEBREAKERS

1. Do you see any fundamental problems with the system of dating as it exists today? What are they?
2. Were the opinions of the guests and host of *Politically Incorrect* surprising to you?

GETTING SERIOUS

1. Read the story of Troy and Jayme (page 27). Could you relate to their situation? Why is it important to define the level of commitment in a relationship before deepening intimacy?
2. If the Little Relationship Principle is God's design for us, will traditional dating as we know it ever *really* work? Why or why not?

BEING REAL

1. How does premature intimacy affect people when a dating relationship ends?
2. Have you experienced an "emotional hook-up" like Josh described or witnessed one in the lives of people around you?
3. How does the Little Relationship Principle help you determine how close you can be as friends with a member of the opposite sex?
4. Are you in a relationship that involves intimacy not matched by commitment? Are you ready to make a change? How will you do that?

JUST FOR GUYS

Have you been guilty of awakening desires in a girl (and yourself) that God means to be left at rest until marriage? How can you choose to avoid such a situation in the future?

JUST FOR GIRLS

If you, like Jayme (page 27), have given your heart and emotions to someone without a long-term commitment, how can you turn from this?

REFLECTION

Chapter 2 is one that I added when I was given the chance to update *I Kissed Dating Goodbye* five years after I first wrote it. It's my attempt to sum up what I consider to be the main problem in dating today.

What is this fundamental problem? It's that we've disconnected romance and commitment. Christian college professor Greg Spencer calls this *emotional fornication*. It's a shocking phrase, but read his explanation below and see if you don't agree that it's an accurate description of what many couples do:

> The privilege of sex requires the lifetime commitment of marriage. Might there be some other aspect of relations that requires the commitment of marriage? I believe so. Just as physical union is meant to be delayed until marriage, emotional loyalty with another person should not be consummated until that time.
>
> "Emotional fornication" refers to the premature expression of loyalty to one another. Like physical fornication, it attempts to live out one of the privileges of marriage without the responsibility of making a lifelong pledge. After having made death-do-us-part promises on their wedding day, the bride and groom now have heavenly permission to be responsible to each other. The Biblical directive is "do not act united until you are formally united." The dangers of premature commitment, like those of premarital sex, stem from snatching a gift of God out of its proper context.[1]

The term *emotional fornication* simply describes how a person might attempt to enjoy intimacy without commitment. This person is, in essence, saying, "God, I can't wait till I'm ready for marriage, so I'm going to snatch this gift of intimacy and enjoy it now."

Are you creeping toward emotional fornication in a relationship? It might not be a dating relationship. Maybe it's just a so-called friendship in which you're getting closer and closer emotionally when you're not willing or able to consider commitment.

Let me encourage you to practice "emotional purity" and to remember the principle we discussed in this chapter: *The joy of intimacy is the reward of commitment.* Until you're ready for commitment, don't steal intimacy.

1. Spencer, Greg. *A Heart for Truth: Taking Your Faith to College* (Grand Rapids, Mich.: Baker Book House, 1993). Used by permission.

The Seven Habits of Highly Defective Dating

Recognizing Dating's Negative Tendencies

CHAPTER AT A GLANCE

This chapter explains how dating can be like a swerving grocery cart—a set of values and attitudes that want to go in a direction different from the one God has mapped out for us. It looks at how self-control by itself isn't enough to solve our problems and why we should instead *replace* this defective "cart" called dating. To help us understand the problems inherent in dating, we examine seven problems:

1. Dating tends to skip the "friendship" stage of a relationship.
2. Dating often mistakes a physical relationship for love.
3. Dating often isolates a couple from other vital relationships.
4. Dating, in many cases, distracts young adults from their primary responsibility of preparing for the future.
5. Dating can cause discontentment with God's gift of singleness.
6. Dating creates an artificial environment for evaluating another person's character.
7. Dating often becomes an end in itself.

We can't solve dating's problems merely by "dating right." Instead of following the way of the world, what we really need is a new attitude.

KEY QUOTE

"We don't find the real beauty of singleness in pursuing romance with as many different people as we want. We find the real beauty in using our freedom to serve God with abandon."

KEY SCRIPTURE

Psalm 119:104: "I gain understanding from your precepts; therefore I hate every wrong path." (Also see Proverbs 15:22 and 1 Thessalonians 4:6.)

GOAL OF DISCUSSION

As we talk about chapter 3, we want to see if we are practicing any of the "Seven Habits of Highly Defective Dating." We should discuss whether we are willing to replace this "swerving cart" called dating and what steps we must take to do so.

ICEBREAKERS

1. Now that you've made it through chapter 3, what do you think of the book so far? Thumbs up or thumbs down?
2. Although Josh covered most of the major problems with our system of dating, what are some additional defective habits you could add to the list?

GETTING SERIOUS

1. Read the story of Garreth and Jenny (pages 41–2). The message that we should "save sex for marriage" is important, but it's not all we need to do. Why?
2. How can dating distract us from the real beauty of singleness—the freedom to serve God with abandon?

BEING REAL

1. Which of the "Seven Habits" could you most relate to? Why?
2. Like Christopher and Stephanie (page 43), have you neglected other pursuits because of a dating relationship? How could you change this?
3. If you are in a relationship where physical intimacy is involved, are you ready to repent? What practical changes do you need to make?
4. Are you willing to relinquish the swerving cart of dating? If not, what is holding you back?

JUST FOR GUYS

What's one practical way you can make friendship with girls your focus instead of romance?

JUST FOR GIRLS

Like Heidi (pages 39–40), have you ever gotten into a romantic situation that "felt right" but should never have happened? How can you avoid situations like this in the future?

REFLECTION

Chapter 3 points out the problems that plague many dating relationships. But this isn't just a finger-wagging session about what's wrong with dating relationships today. We're not just saying no to the *defective,* but yes to the *effective.*

Look at the "Seven Habits of Defective Dating" from that perspective, and you'll see what I mean. Turn each problem inside out and you will realize that by rejecting the defective, you're welcoming God's best for your life. Look at what you're saying yes to:

1. I reject defective dating that tends to skip the friendship stage of a relationship, and I choose to build my future marriage on the solid foundation of friendship with my spouse.
2. I reject defective dating that mistakes a physical a relationship for love, and I choose purity and the clarity that comes in a relationship undistracted by premarital physical involvement.
3. I reject defective dating that isolates me from other vital relationships, and I'm saying yes to the joy, wisdom, and godly perspective that comes from investing in family and other friends.
4. I reject defective dating that distracts me from my primary responsibility of preparation, and I choose to glorify God and serve my future spouse by using this time in my life to prepare for the future.
5. I reject defective dating that causes discontentment with God's gift of singleness, and I embrace the contentment that comes with a heart of gratefulness and an attitude that seeks to make the most of today.
6. I reject defective dating that creates an artificial environment for evaluating another person's character, and I choose to get to know my future spouse in a setting that lets us both see who we really are and what our true character is.

7. I reject dating that becomes an end in itself, and I choose a healthy
   romantic relationship that bridges friendship and marriage and to
   either move purposefully towards commitment or just be friends
   with the other person.

We don't "kiss dating goodbye" because we're afraid of relationships
but because we want something better—a lifestyle of purposeful singleness that allows us to make the most of today and prepare for tomorrow.

CHAPTER FOUR

Counterculture Romance

Five Attitude Changes to Help
You Avoid Defective Dating

CHAPTER AT A GLANCE

The goal of chapter 4 is to give us new thinking to adopt toward dating. We want to break away from dating's negative habits by taking on a new attitude regarding love, purity, and singleness. These new attitudes are:

1. Every relationship is an opportunity to model Christ's love.
2. My unmarried years are a gift from God.
3. I don't need to pursue a romantic relationship before I'm ready for marriage.
4. I cannot "own" someone outside of marriage.
5. I will avoid situations that could compromise the purity of my body or mind.

Through these new attitudes, we are challenged to set aside our romantic ambitions until it is time to pursue them on God's terms and in His time. We can trust God to give us His best, but first we must be willing to give Him ours.

KEY QUOTE

"Rejecting the old attitude is the natural response not only to the evident problems in dating, but more important, to the high calling we've received from God."

KEY SCRIPTURE

Ephesians 4:22–24: "You were taught, with regard to your former way of life, to put off your old self, which is being corrupted by its deceitful desires; to be made new in the attitude of your minds; and to put on the new self, created to be like God in true righteousness and holiness." (Also see Matthew 6:33 and Hebrews 12:1.)

GOAL OF DISCUSSION

The purpose of this chapter is to encourage us to embrace the new attitudes that help us leave dating behind. How should we think and act differently so we can receive God's best for our lives?

ICEBREAKERS

1. What's another area of your life (besides dating) where you could use a new attitude?
2. How much has your perspective on dating changed since reading the first four chapters?

GETTING SERIOUS

1. In this chapter Josh writes, "You and I will never experience God's best...until we give God our all" (page 55) How does this apply to dating relationships?
2. Read Hebrews 12:1. In light of this verse, why is it important that we adopt a new attitude toward dating?

BEING REAL

1. Which of the five new attitudes is the most radical for you? What radical action do you need to take?
2. The fifth new attitude (page 53) says, "I will avoid situations that could compromise the purity of my body or mind." What situations do you need to avoid?
3. If you are in an intimate relationship that lacks commitment, how can you adopt a new attitude toward that relationship?
4. Are you ready to give God your all? If not, what "marbles" are you still holding on to?

JUST FOR GUYS

The second new attitude is, "My unmarried years are a gift from God." What's one practical way that embracing this perspective would affect the way you spend your time?

JUST FOR GIRLS

How can you, like Bethany (page 50), turn from flirtatiousness and model Christ's love to others?

REFLECTION

How do you close a letter to a friend? Some people write "Sincerely" or "Love"; I write "Doit4Jesus!" at the end of mine. I take it from 1 Corinthians 10:31, which says, "So whether you eat or drink or whatever you do, do it all for the glory of God." It's a way to remind myself that no matter what I'm doing, it should be for God and His glory.

And that's at the heart of the five new attitudes listed in chapter 4. They each stem from the calling we have as Christians to live for God's glory. We need to see every part of our lives (including romance) as belonging to God.

"The question is not whether or not to date," one reader wrote me. "The question is, are we willing to submit everything to the control of Christ? Dating just happens to be at the top of the list of what comes between Christians and our God."

He's exactly right. And anything that comes between us and God begins to take God's place.

Another guy understood this principle. He wrote me this note:

I received *I Kissed Dating Goodbye* a few weeks ago from my pastor. I must say when I first heard the title, I was discouraged. You see, I'm thirty-three years old, and I'm still single. My pastor knows I've been desiring to get married for a long time, and by the sound of the title I thought he was telling me to give up looking for a girl and be content being single. But I'm happy to tell you that after reading your book, I don't think that was his intention at all. I think he used it to reemphasize what he's been telling me for the last three years—namely,

"Don't make a girl an idol." I have such a yearning to be married that I'm afraid I put a girl above God. I know now that I have to always keep God as my "first love."

This guy and his pastor have it right. Anything that becomes more important than God is an idol. We need a change of attitude that places God first in our lives and sees our every action as an expression of love for Him that brings Him glory.

CHAPTER FIVE

Looking Up "Love" in God's Dictionary

Learning the True Definition of Love

CHAPTER AT A GLANCE

This chapter opens with the story of two very different couples, illustrating the distinction between the world's definition of love and God's true love. All of the negative problems associated with dating can be linked to adopting a fallen world's attitudes toward love. We need to gain God's perspective and remember that as Christians we're "models" of God's love to the world. The chapter shows us three lies in the world's pattern for love:

1. The world's deceptions flow from the belief that love is primarily for the fulfillment of self, but true love is defined by serving others and living for the glory of God. Jesus demonstrated this kind of love by dying on the cross.
2. The world claims that love is based on feeling, but true love is based on obedience to God and service to others (John 14:15).
3. The world tells us that love is unpredictable and beyond our control, but true love is a choice we must make, just as Jesus chose to love us.

The chapter also shows that true love must be sincere (Romans 12:9) and based on commitment. We must stop trying to fit God's ideas into the lifestyles society has defined for us and allow His values and attitudes to redefine the way we live.

KEY QUOTE

"We cannot love as God loves and date as the world dates."

KEY SCRIPTURE

1 Corinthians 13:4–8: "Love is patient, love is kind. It does not envy, it does not boast, it is not proud. It is not rude, it is not self-seeking, it is not easily angered, it keeps no record of wrongs. Love does not delight in evil but rejoices with the truth. It always protects, always trusts, always hopes, always perseveres. Love never fails." (Also see Matthew 16:24; John 13:34–35; 14:15; 15:13; Romans 12:9; 1 John 2:16; and 4:16.)

GOAL OF DISCUSSION

Our discussion should help us see the lies behind the world's definition of love and how they have influenced us. Are we willing to reject the world's pattern of love and give up dating? How can we model Christ's love in our relationships?

ICEBREAKERS

1. What are some examples of ads, music, or movies that promote a worldly or unbiblical view of love?
2. In one word, describe your reaction to Eric and Leslie's story (pages 60–1)? What do you think about not kissing until your wedding day?

GETTING SERIOUS

1. Why do people like to talk about love being beyond their control? How is this attitude different from the definition of love found in 1 Corinthians 13?
2. Share some ways that Jesus is our example of perfect love.

BEING REAL

1. Did you recognize changes you need to make after reading the first four chapters? What have been the results?
2. Both Jeff and Gloria (pages 59–60) and Eric and Leslie (pages 60–1) described their actions as motivated by love. Which more closely describes the way you define love? Why?
3. If biblical love is what we are meant to be "wearing," what would people who observe you say that love is?
4. How does a biblical definition of love nullify dating? Why do you

agree or disagree? Are you going to change anything about the way you're living?

JUST FOR GUYS

On page 69, Josh lists some questions to help evaluate our motives for relationships. He asks, "What am I seeking that couldn't be found in a friendship?" How would you answer that question?

JUST FOR GIRLS

What's one way you are tempted to be manipulative and insincere in your relationships with guys? How are you going to practice biblical love instead?

REFLECTION

Have you ever mispronounced a word? Recently I displayed my ignorance when I mispronounced a word of French origin in front of three thousand people. The person who kindly pointed out my error afterward said, "You've probably seen it written more than you've heard it pronounced." He was right. I'd read the word, understood what it meant, but didn't know how to say it correctly.

My mispronunciation is a fitting analogy for the way many of us handle the word *love*. We've read about it, watched countless movies expounding on it, and listened to our share of songs extolling it. But have we ever actually seen it demonstrated?

Jesus' close friend John didn't think most of us have. That's why he carefully pointed to the Cross as the one perfect demonstration of love: "This is how we know what love is: Jesus Christ laid down his life for us" (1 John 3:16).

How can we know what love is? "This is how," John says, and he points us to the place the sinless Savior hung in our place, receiving the wrath of God.

How can I know God loves me? "This is how," John says, and again the Cross is the irrefutable evidence of God's individual, specific love for us. The Cross shows us what our sins deserve. It shows us God's justice in punishing all sin. But most wonderfully it shows God's love. He showed us mercy—He died in our place.

When we look up *love* in God's dictionary, we find the Cross as the first definition. In it we see that true love *can* be known, it *can* be experienced, it *has* been demonstrated.

CHAPTER SIX

The Right Thing at the Wrong Time Is the Wrong Thing

How to Keep Impatience from Robbing You of the Gift of Singleness

CHAPTER AT A GLANCE

This chapter shows that *when* we pursue romance is a major factor in determining whether or not dating is appropriate for us. And we can only determine the appropriate time to pursue romance when we understand God's purpose for singleness and trust *His* timing for relationships. Modern culture thrives on immediate gratification, but God's Word teaches that there are appointed seasons for everything in our lives, including relationships.

Three principles are given to help adjust wrong attitudes about the timing of relationships:

1. *The right thing at the wrong time is the wrong thing.* A good thing taken out of its appropriate season can actually be destructive.
2. *We don't need to shop for something we can't afford.* Before two people are ready for the responsibility of commitment, they should content themselves with friendship and wait for romance and intimacy.
3. *Any season of singleness is a gift from God.* God has created this season as an unparalleled opportunity for growth and service. We shouldn't let it slip by.

Waiting for God's timing requires trust in His goodness. We develop patience as we trust that God denies us good things in the present only because He has something better for us in the future. Waiting for God's timing also requires strength. This strength comes from God alone. His strength and grace will sustain us through any circumstance.

KEY QUOTE

"Just as spring's role is different from that of fall, so each of the seasons of our lives has a different emphasis, focus, and beauty.... We cannot skip ahead to experience the riches of another life season any more than a farmer can rush the spring."

KEY SCRIPTURE

1 Corinthians 7:32 (*The Message*): "The time and energy that married people spend on caring for and nurturing each other, the unmarried can spend in becoming whole and holy instruments of God." (Also see Ecclesiastes 3:1–8; Jeremiah 29:11–13; Philippians 4:11, 13; and 1 Timothy 6:6.)

GOAL OF DISCUSSION

We want to determine if impatience is motivating our relationships. How can we view our singleness as a gift and trust God's timing?

ICEBREAKERS

1. Which kid could you relate to in the marshmallow test example (pages 81–3)?
2. When was the last time you had to wait for something, and how did you respond?

GETTING SERIOUS

1. What are common, everyday situations in which you wish you could just "pull the thread" and escape? How has your perspective changed since reading Peter's story (pages 75–6)?
2. Read Ecclesiastes 3:1–8. How can the biblical principle of seasons help us to be patient?

BEING REAL

1. Is impatience motivating you in dating relationships? What are you impatient for?

2. Do you relate to a member of the opposite sex as if he or she is somebody else's future husband or wife? What would this look like?
3. Before reading this chapter, did you think of singleness as a gift or a punishment? How do you feel *after* reading the chapter?
4. Is there an area of your life where you are having difficulty trusting God? How would faith in His goodness help you to be content?

JUST FOR GUYS

On page 80, Josh shares the quote, "Don't do something about your sin-glehood—do something *with* it!" What are you doing with your singlehood?

JUST FOR GIRLS

How does pressure from others affect your contentment with single-ness? How should you respond?

REFLECTION

I read a plaque in a friend's home that captures the essence of chapter 6. It said, "Contentment is not the fulfillment of what you want, but the realization of how much you already have."

Contentment is not a destination. We don't arrive at it when we become a certain age, get married, achieve our goals, or reach a specific bank balance. Contentment is a state of gratefulness before God. Until we understand that, we'll waste our time attempting to "arrive" at a place of contentment only to discover it's just beyond our grasp—always "tomorrow."

Most of us can relate to the "contentment on our terms" mindset. In the area of relationships, we're perfectly willing to be content as soon as God brings along our husband or wife. All God needs to do is tell us who this person is and when we'll meet him or her and we'll be happy. But that's not true contentment, is it? True contentment is being more aware of how much we already have and trusting that God will provide the grace we need to persevere, no matter how difficult our circumstances might be.

That was the apostle Paul's secret. In Philippians 4:11–13, he wrote, "I have learned to be content whatever the circumstances. I know what it is to be in need, and I know what it is to have plenty. I have learned the secret of being content in any and every situation, whether well fed or hungry, whether living in plenty or in want. I can do everything through him who gives me strength."

For Paul, the knowledge that God is sovereign and will sustain those who trust Him was the secret to contentment. Apply it to your situation. Are you content even if a relationship is something you have to wait months or years for? Do you believe that the "everything" God's strength will help you with includes waiting on His timing for romance? Do you believe that God's strength can meet you in your present circumstances and help you be obedient right where you are? If you do, then you've found the secret to contentment—something that no one can take from you.

So choose to be content. Choose to focus on all God has given you. Maybe it's not as much as someone else has, but that's not the point. Count *your* blessings. And if all you can think of is that He died for your sins and has given you an eternity with Him in heaven, that's enough to keep you rejoicing all your days.

CHAPTER SEVEN

The Direction of Purity

How to Get on the Road to Righteousness

CHAPTER AT A GLANCE

This chapter challenges us to stop viewing purity as a line that we shouldn't cross and start viewing it as a direction—a persistent, determined pursuit of righteousness. This direction starts in the heart, and we express it in a lifestyle that flees opportunities for compromise.

We read about how King David, by taking small steps toward sin, ended up committing adultery and murder. The same is true for us. If we choose the direction of purity but fail to support it in practical decisions of where, when, and with whom we choose to be, we'll end up in compromise.

We're given three principles to help us maintain the direction of purity:

1. Respect the deep significance of physical intimacy. Refuse to steal these privileges before marriage.
2. Set your standards too high. Cut off the opportunity for sin at its root, and flee from even the slightest possibility of compromise.
3. Make the purity of others a priority. For guys this means we must start being "warriors" standing guard over girls' hearts. For girls this means doing all we can to guard our brothers' eyes by being careful that we don't act, glance, or dress in ways designed to attract attention or show off.

Purity doesn't happen by accident; it requires obedience to God. But this obedience is not burdensome or overbearing. We have only to consider the alternative of impurity to see the beauty, power, and protection of walking in God's will.

KEY QUOTE

"We cannot simultaneously explore the boundaries of purity and pursue righteousness—they point us in opposite directions."

KEY SCRIPTURE

2 Timothy 2:22: "Flee the evil desires of youth, and pursue righteousness, faith, love and peace, along with those who call on the Lord out of a pure heart." (Also see Psalm 24:3–4; Proverbs 7:25–27; Matthew 5:8; Colossians 3:5; Hebrews 10:24; and James 1:14–15.)

GOAL OF DISCUSSION

The aim of our discussion is to provoke us to pursue purity as a direction. What are our convictions regarding purity, and what areas of compromise do we need to flee? How can we serve others in their pursuit of purity?

ICEBREAKERS

1. When you think of purity, what kinds of words or images come to mind?
2. What are some other stories of people who pursue purity and righteousness? How can their examples inspire us?

GETTING SERIOUS

1. Josh talks about the deep significance of physical intimacy (pages 92–5). Why is this deeply significant?
2. In this chapter, Josh says, "We esteem purity too little and desire it too late." What do you think he means by this?

BEING REAL

1. Josh writes that in the area of purity "we often have pricked consciences but unchanged lives" (page 88). What's an example of this in your own life? In what way should you change?

2. Like King David, what seemingly small steps are you taking toward impurity? How did this story affect you? Is there an area of sin or impurity that you need to repent of?
3. How can you set your standards "too high" in this area?
4. Girls, share some practical ways the guys can help guard your hearts.

JUST FOR GUYS

Josh writes on page 91 that "the direction of purity begins within; you must support it in practical everyday decisions of where, when, and with whom you choose to be." What's one practical decision you need to make?

JUST FOR GIRLS

Are your clothes designed to attract attention or to protect the guys from stumbling? What clothes need to be replaced?

REFLECTION

The final section of chapter 7 talks about how we need to make the purity of others our responsibility. That's not always easy, is it? We can wind up looking prudish or "out of it." Sometimes it involves telling people what they don't want to hear. Let me share a story from my own experience.

A few years ago I was a guest speaker at a Christian music festival in Pennsylvania called Creation. I was there to speak on the topic of purity in one of the seminars taking place on the side of a wooded hill. Minutes before I spoke, I started to get nervous. Part of my message contained a challenge to girls to dress modestly. I had shared it many times, but always in nice, air-conditioned churches where the audience was fully clothed. It was a different story at an outdoor festival in the middle of summer. Here under the hot sun modesty was literally "not cool."

The area around me was swarming with sweaty people trying to find solace from bottled water and snow cones. Many of the girls wore short shorts and bikini tops. The thought of talking about modesty to a crowd dressed like this made me feel sick.

I knelt down next to a tree, opened my notebook, and removed the page that contained the section on modesty. *I don't need to share this part,* I thought. *It will offend them. The message will be better without it.* Then the justifications started rolling. The sinful part of me that wants every-one to like me started to justify leaving out that section. *They'll think you're judgmental if you say that,* it reasoned. *They'll roll their eyes at you. They'll snicker.*

But a moment later my conscience kicked in: *You're more worried about impressing this crowd than you are about pleasing God.* I hesitated. With a groan, I put the page back in my notebook. *God,* I prayed, *I want to say what You want me to say.*

The message went well. When I came to the dreaded section, I was honest with the crowd and told them my temptation to leave it out. "But you know what?" I said. "I want to be more afraid of God than I am of you." To my surprise they applauded. Then they listened.

"You really have no clue," I said to the girls, "how hard it is for a guy to look at you with purity in his heart when you're dressed immod-estly. If you could get inside a guy's head for a day—or even ten minutes!—I believe it would significantly change your wardrobe. And if it didn't, what would that say about your heart? It's your heart that I want to encourage you to examine. I'm not here to start measuring skirt lengths. The question is, what is your heart's motive? Do you want to stir up lust in a guy?"

I closed with this encouragement: "Ladies, we live in a day and age when you're bombarded with the message that your value is in the way you look—your body and your appearance. All I can say is that if living a life of obedience before God in the way you dress meant that you never caught the second glance of another guy, it would be worth it. Because your value is not in the attention of any guy—your value is in the fact that Christ loves you and died for you and that you are His daughter. That's your value! And your true beauty comes from a heart and life surrendered to Him. That is true beauty!"

Afterward countless guys and girls came up and thanked me for sharing that material. I cringe when I think of how close I came to dis-obeying God and leaving it out. For me, that message was a way to watch out for other people's purity. You'll have your own opportunities. Don't let them slip by—be bold! Let's obey God and love our brothers and sisters by making their purity our responsibility.

CHAPTER EIGHT

A Cleansed Past: The Room

How Jesus Can Redeem Your Past

CHAPTER AT A GLANCE

In this chapter, Josh shares a dream he had called "The Room." He dedicates it to those who after studying the importance of purity might feel discouraged because of past sin.

In the dream, Josh is in a room filled with index-card files. In each file, his every good and bad deed is recorded. As he stands facing the horror of his many sins, Jesus enters the room and begins to sign His name in His blood over Josh's on each card. The dream ends as Jesus leads Josh out of the room, leaving the door unlocked. There were still more cards to be written.

This dream is a powerful illustration of Jesus taking our sin upon Himself. Because no one can stand completely pure before Him, God sent His Son, Jesus Christ, to pay our debt. Through His death on the cross, Christ's righteousness has been transferred to us. In God's eyes we are spotless, pure, and justified. Because of Jesus, a lifetime of purity awaits us.

KEY QUOTE

"Then He got up and walked back to the wall of files. Starting at one end of the room, He took out a file and, one by one, began to sign His name over mine on each card.... It was written with His blood."

KEY SCRIPTURE

Hebrews 8:12: "For I will forgive their wickedness and will remember their sins no more." (Also see Romans 13:12–14.)

GOAL OF DISCUSSION

Our discussion of "The Room" is to remind us that Jesus' blood has covered *all* our sins. Because He has paid our debt, we don't need to live in the past anymore. We also want to ask, "What sins do we need to receive His forgiveness for? How can we move forward into a lifetime of purity?"

ICEBREAKERS

1. Describe in one word the emotion you felt after reading "The Room."
2. Josh talks about statements such as "Jesus loves me" that can become familiar to us. What other Christian truths could become meaningless because we've heard them so many times?

GETTING SERIOUS

1. What specific, ungodly files do we continually add cards to in the dating game?
2. If Christ has promised to no longer remember our sins, how should that affect *our* memories?

BEING REAL

1. Are there sinful areas of your life you haven't repented of? Take some time right now to ask God's forgiveness and receive Christ's purity.
2. Let's do a little exercise. This is not meant to call up bad memories but to help you understand Christ's forgiveness: Think of your worst card. Then remind yourself that Jesus has covered even that card with His blood. When God looks at you, He no longer sees that sin, but Christ's righteousness. You are forgiven and free to live a life of purity.
3. How has reading about Josh's dream helped you deal with past regret? In what ways have you received fresh motivation for purity?
4. What do you think about more often: past sins or Christ's blood that covers them? When you are tempted to think about your past, how can you remind yourself of God's forgiveness?

JUST FOR GUYS

Read Romans 13:12–14. How did "The Room" motivate you to stop thinking about how to gratify the "desires of the sinful nature"?

JUST FOR GIRLS

How can Christ's forgiveness help you deal with shame from past sins?

REFLECTION

A prayer…

I went to The Room again today, Lord.
There's part of me that doesn't like to visit.
There are so many moments, so many careless words,
so many selfish actions I want to forget.
But it's no longer a place of horror.
I went to be reminded of all that You've done for me.
I don't ever want to forget the crushing weight of bearing my own sin, of
having my name on each of those cards.
I don't ever want to forget what it's like to be lost
so that I'll never cease to be grateful for being found.
Forgive me, Jesus, but sometimes I grow so
familiar with Your grace that I take it for granted.
Standing before those files with my every sin recorded, I see what a wretch
I am, and Your grace is once again amazing.
I learned something today, too.
I realized that Your grace not only covers
my sin but also makes possible my obedience.
I pulled out a few card files of things I've done right: "Encouragement I've
Given," "Times I Served Others," and "Temptations Resisted."
I saw Your name written on those, too.
I think I half expected to see my own name.
What a fool I am! It suddenly hit me that everything
good I've been able to do has been by Your grace.
I couldn't serve, I couldn't love, I couldn't be patient
without Your grace upholding me and Your Spirit guiding me.
I stood there and cried again. They were happy tears.
I stood there aware that I had nothing to brag
about except Your work in my life.

Your servant Paul said, "May I never boast except
in the cross of our Lord Jesus Christ" (Galatians 6:14).
I see what he meant now. Everything I have, You've given me.
You made possible the forgiveness of my sins.
You give me the power to obey.
I have nothing to boast in—no achievement, no righteousness,
no merit—except for Your finished work.
Thank You, Jesus.

Starting with a Clean Slate

Five Important Steps for Getting on Track with God's Plan

CHAPTER AT A GLANCE

In this chapter, we read the story of a builder whose most valuable tool was his nail puller. He had learned the hard way that when you realize you've made a mistake, it's better to "pull a few nails" and start over than to continue on the wrong course.

Chapter 9 gives us five steps that will provide a solid foundation for a godly lifestyle:

1. *Start with a clean slate.* This means repenting of any sinful attitudes and behaviors in our relationships. This might mean refocusing relationships are headed off course or ending those we know are wrong.
2. *Make your parents your teammates.* We need to humbly involve our parents and other godly individuals who can keep us accountable, provide encouragement, and give us correction and counsel.
3. *Establish clear guidelines.* We develop these guidelines with the people who can help us stay on course.
4. *Check to see who's whispering in your ear.* This means making sure that the things that influence us—music, books, TV, friends—are encouraging and supporting godly standards and beliefs.
5. *Season your conviction with humility.* This means being humble when we tell people about our decision not to date—recognizing that we don't have all the answers, but that we believe this is God's call for our life.

KEY QUOTE

"When you realize you've made a mistake, the best thing you can do is tear down the wall and start over.... For many, getting things right will require us to first tear down what's wrong. In some cases, that means bringing wrong relationships to an end."

KEY SCRIPTURE

Ecclesiastes 3:1, 3: "There is a time for everything, and a season for every activity under heaven...a time to tear down and a time to build."

GOAL OF DISCUSSION

Our objective for this discussion is to examine our relationships. What faulty attitudes and patterns of dating do we need to tear down? What steps can we take to ensure that our future relationships are built on a solid foundation?

ICEBREAKERS

1. If you were invited to Stephen's birthday party, what "tool" would you give him? Why?
2. Have you ever tried to complete a project that had a fundamental flaw? How did it turn out?

GETTING SERIOUS

1. Why is repentance the *first* step in seeking to build a godly lifestyle? What would be the result if we tried to pursue a new life without first turning away from sin?
2. What are the benefits of having your parents (or a trusted Christian mentor) as your teammates?

BEING REAL

1. Josh writes, "Obedience today will save you a lot of sorrow and regret tomorrow" (page 114). What do you need to do *today* in order to avoid regret and pain tomorrow?
2. Do people or other influences tempt you to compromise or be discontent? What do you need to tune out or turn off?
3. What boundaries do you need to set to help you avoid temptation?
4. Is there a relationship you need to either break off or "refocus"? What are some of the obstacles to doing this? How can you overcome them?

JUST FOR GUYS

If you need to end a relationship that is wrong, how can you humbly break up?

JUST FOR GIRLS

What is one way you can involve the wisdom and accountability of your parents (or a trusted Christian mentor) in your life?

REFLECTION

God loves obedience. Not talk, not good intentions, but obedience. He loves it when we take Him at His word—take Him seriously—and do what He's told us to do. It's much easier to speak theoretically about living for God and nod our heads in agreement with what the Bible says than it is to actually do it. But if we would be lovers of God, then we must be "doers" of His will.

I'm glad to say that there are many of these kind of Christians around today. I've had the privilege of meeting many guys and girls who have taken the difficult step of ending a relationship that they knew was wrong.

One such example is a girl in my church named Roxanne. When she became a Christian a few years ago, she'd been in a relationship for eight years.

"It was my entire life," she says. "I was afraid my life would be empty and hopeless without my boyfriend."

But Roxanne made the decision to obey her new Lord no matter what the cost and broke off the relationship. Two years later she's thriving in our church, has strong friendships with Christian girls and guys, and is introducing others to Christ—all things she couldn't have done had she failed to obey.

What's your situation? Maybe your wrong relationship is only eight *days* old. Don't wait to change your course.

First John 5:3 sums up the message of chapter 9 perfectly: "This is love for God: to obey his commands. And his commands are not burdensome."

Do you want to love God? Then obey Him. Your obedience says that you trust Him, that His ways are good, that you want to please Him more than you want anything else, that He is your first love.

And the beautiful thing is that when you obey God's commands, you'll find that instead of being harsh and heavy, they're "easy" and "light." In following them, you'll find rest for your soul (Matthew 11:29–30).

CHAPTER TEN

Just Friends in a Just-Do-It World

Keys for Keeping Your Relationships with the Opposite Sex out of the "Romantic Zone"

CHAPTER AT A GLANCE

Being "just friends" with the opposite sex can be difficult and confusing. In this chapter, we learn that we must recognize the limitations of guy-girl friendships. While these friendships can be good, there are boundaries. We're given four steps that can help us maintain healthy friendships with the opposite sex:

1. *We need to understand the difference between friendship and intimacy.* Friendship is about something other than the two people in the relationship—intimacy is about each other.
2. *When spending time with members of the opposite sex, we need to be inclusive, not exclusive.* This means including others instead of isolating ourselves with just one person. Inclusion must stem from a sincere desire to involve as many people as possible in fellowship and service.
3. *We need to make a priority of same-sex relationships.* Friendships with the same sex can last a lifetime. Throughout our lives, they'll be an important source of encouragement, counsel, perspective, and accountability.
4. *Seek opportunities to serve, not to be entertained.* In service, we find true friendship and can know our friends in a deeper way than ever before.

We have to fight for and guard our friendships. We can do this by respecting the limitations of guy-girl relationships and relating to others within the framework given by God's Word.

KEY QUOTE

"The key to friendship is a common goal or object on which both companions focus. It can be an athletic pursuit, a hobby, faith, or music, but it's something *outside* of them. As soon as the two people involved focus on *the relationship,* it has moved beyond friendship."

KEY SCRIPTURE

Romans 12:10–11: "Be devoted to one another in brotherly love. Honor one another above yourselves. Never be lacking in zeal, but keep your spiritual fervor, serving the Lord." (Also see Proverbs 25:16 and 1 Timothy 5:2.)

GOAL OF DISCUSSION

We want to discuss how to have meaningful friendships with the opposite sex without crossing the line of intimacy. In what ways can we serve others instead of seeking our own selfish desires?

ICEBREAKERS

1. In Proverbs 25:16, Solomon uses honey as an example of something that is good, but can be harmful if you have too much. What's another illustration of this principle?
2. Have you ever had a similar experience to Josh's where you were the "third wheel" in a dating relationship? We're sure it was a lot of fun—tell us about it!

GETTING SERIOUS

1. What desires—good and bad—can push us beyond friendship? What does the Bible say about these desires?
2. Josh makes the point that "our cultural obsession with entertainment is really just an expression of selfishness" (page 135). How does this selfishness affect our relationships?

BEING REAL

1. What are some indications (in your heart or by your actions) that you have crossed the line from friendship to intimacy? How can you pursue friendship instead?
2. Share an experience like the one about Josh and Chelsea of friendship gone too far. What would you do differently?

3. Are you isolating yourself with just one person? Who do you need to include in your friendship? How can you do this practically?
4. What is one way you can serve with others this week, instead of seeking entertainment and selfish satisfaction from your relationships? Be prepared to share your experience during the next discussion.

JUST FOR GUYS

Read 1 Timothy 5:2. If you are to treat women "as sisters, with absolute purity," how should you change so this describes you *absolutely?*

JUST FOR GIRLS

How can you serve guys in practical ways without crossing the line into more than friendship?

REFLECTION

I received this hilarious e-mail from a young reader:

> I'm having a problem with a girl at school. She nags me all the time and I really want it to stop. She has this crush on me, but I dislike her. What should I do?
>
> I've already tried avoiding her, not speaking to her, and running away, but she won't stop. It's like the Energizer Bunny—it keeps going and going and going.
>
> She's just not my type. She has made me change my favorite verse from Romans 8:28 to Proverbs 21:19, which says, "Better to be in the desert than with a vexing woman." I'm a seventh-grader at Cedar Bluff Middle and in need of serious help. Please pray for me, and please reply ASAP.

I wrote back and encouraged him not to be distracted by dating, but also to be a gentleman. "Be humble. Just because you don't like this girl doesn't mean you should be unkind," I said.

An important ingredient to friendships with the opposite sex is humility. Whether you're in seventh grade being "chased" by a suitor or a college freshman being asked why *you* aren't chasing someone, you need an attitude of humility.

Whenever we set a high standard in an area of our life, we face the temptation of being impressed with ourselves. "Boy, I'm really giving a lot to the church. How generous I am!" While we may be doing something that is pleasing to God, this attitude is one that He hates.

Take a moment to read Luke 18:9–14. It's the Parable of the Pharisee and the Tax Collector. One man was self-righteous and proud of his own works. The other was humble and aware of his need for divine mercy. Jesus told the story for those "who were confident of their own righteousness and looked down on everybody else" (Luke 18:9). Does that describe you? After you read the original version from Luke, read this version, modified to reflect the topic at hand:

> Two young men slipped into a quiet chapel to pray. One had been a Christian since age five and was known in his church for his commitment not to date and never to kiss a girl till he was married. The other was a ladies' man with a reputation for using the many girls he'd dated. The first stood up in front of the altar and prayed about himself: "God, I thank you that I am not like other men—immoral, evildoers, adulterers—or even like this guy who has dated half the town. I'm a virgin and have never touched a woman."
>
> But the other young man stood at a distance. He was so aware of his own sinfulness that he couldn't bring himself to look up to heaven. He cried hot tears and said, "God, have mercy on me, a sinner."

When Jesus shared the original parable, he told his listeners that the second man who cried out for mercy, not the first, went home justified before God. He closed by saying, "For everyone who exalts himself will be humbled, and he who humbles himself will be exalted" (Luke 18:14).

Self-righteousness is not only displeasing to God, it's just plain ludicrous. You and I have *no* righteousness in ourselves; no one does (Romans 3:9–20). The only righteousness we can have before God is the righteousness given to us by Jesus Christ (Philippians 3:8–9). This knowledge can keep us from looking down on others who have different standards than we do. It can help us when we have to adjust the focus of a relationship that has stepped over the line of friendship. No matter how many good deeds we do or how high our standards for dating are, we're still sinners in need of God's grace. It's easy to be humble when we remember that.

CHAPTER ELEVEN

Guard Your Heart

How to Fight the Pollutants of Lust, Infatuation, and Self-Pity

CHAPTER AT A GLANCE

This chapter shows the importance of guarding our hearts. First, we must understand our hearts are naturally sinful. They often want what is wrong. We have to guard our hearts as if they were bound criminals who would like to break free and knock us over the head. Second, our hearts can easily be contaminated. We must guard them from wrong attitudes, longings, and desires as if they were pure spring water from which we want to drink.

We look at three "pollutants" that we must especially guard against when it comes to relationships:

1. *Infatuation*—which makes another human, instead of God, the object of our longing. We must understand that no human relationship can ever completely fulfill us.
2. *Lust*—which craves something sexually that God has forbidden. To fight lust, we have to detest it with the same intensity that God does.
3. *Self-pity*—which uses feelings as an excuse to turn away from God and exalt our own needs. To combat self-pity, we must refrain from comparing, redirect our feelings into compassion and service to others, and allow feelings of loneliness to draw us closer to God.

The work of watching over our hearts is never done. But God's strength can help see us through the upheavals of our emotions. He will sustain us as we trust in Him.

KEY QUOTE

"When we think 'heart,' we picture cutesy, red, cutout valentines. But often, if we'd really examine our hearts, we'd find lies, selfishness, lust, envy, and pride. And that's the abridged list! The effect is like discovering your sweet old grandmother's picture on the FBI's Most Wanted list at the post office."

KEY SCRIPTURE

Proverbs 4:23: "Above all else, guard your heart, for it is the wellspring of life." (Also see Job 31:1; Psalm 51:10; 86:11; Jeremiah 17:9; Matthew 5:28; Hebrews 7:25; and 1 John 2:15–16; 3:20.)

GOAL OF DISCUSSION

The goal of our discussion is to honestly talk about the deceitfulness of our hearts. Are we being diligent to keep our hearts pure? In what ways do infatuation, lust, and self-pity corrupt them? How can we guard our hearts?

ICEBREAKERS

1. What's a New Year's resolution you've made and quickly abandoned?
2. Give an example from everyday life of something that can feel right but isn't always wise.

GETTING SERIOUS

1. Why can infatuation be a sinful response to attraction? What should we do about it?
2. Read 1 John 3:20. How can this verse provide us with strength and hope as we seek to guard our hearts?

BEING REAL

1. If purity were a point on a compass, which direction would you say you are headed? Straight toward it? Veering off course?
2. As with Julie's scenario (page 141), what's a situation in which it's dangerous for you to trust your feelings or emotions? What could happen if you do?

3. Josh writes that "self-pity is the worship of our circumstances" (page 147). In what area of your life are you tempted toward self-pity?

4. Are you making the same mistake as the town council in the story about the Keeper of the Spring (pages 142–3)? What are the impure things you need to remove from your life?

JUST FOR GUYS

Are you disgusted by the lust in your own heart? In what specific ways do you need to avoid temptation?

JUST FOR GIRLS

What things do you do that feed self-pity in your heart? What should you do instead?

REFLECTION

If I had to rate the three "heart pollutants" examined in chapter 11, lust would be enemy number one. I'm currently working on my third book and it will be about how to overcome this sin. I hate lust, and I battle it daily.

One of my favorite preachers, John Piper, helped me understand lust with this simple equation: "Lust is a sexual desire minus honor and holiness."[1] Sexual desire, he explains, is a perfectly good thing created by God for a husband and wife's enjoyment. But when we lust, we take this good thing and remove from it honor toward fellow humans and reverence for God.

This definition helps me understand what's taking place when I lust after a girl. I'm dishonoring her—treating her as an object instead of as a person created in God's image. And second, I'm shutting out of my life the reality of a holy God.

I tend to think of lust as a guy problem, but girls struggle, too. Thankfully, God's grace is just as available to help the ladies conquer temptation as it is for us guys.

Recently, a girl wrote and shared her story with me. Tina (not her real name) participated in different camps every summer, and seemingly every time she'd develop a crush on one of the guys. One summer she was at a swimming camp in Southern California. "I tend to become instantly attracted to someone," she wrote. "This summer's situation proved to be no different."

It started as soon as she walked off the plane.

"I was greeted at the airport by a friendly group of nice-looking college guys," she said. "Over the next two days, I found myself looking for one in particular. I wanted to talk to him during meals, walk with him on errands, or ride in the van he was driving. Wherever he was, I wanted to be in his presence."

All this would appear innocent to a casual observer, but as Tina admitted, her heart was full of ungodly desires. God reminded Tina of the story I share in chapter 11 about the homosexual men who whistled at me.

"The response in your mind was disgust," Tina wrote. "God's response to you was that your heterosexual lust was just as disgusting to Him."

God used that story to bring conviction to Tina's heart.

"I recalled your story and my situation," she said. "I immediately turned my feelings of lust over to God. I asked God to challenge me to glorify Him in my interactions and behavior. From that point on, I was not as attracted to the person in a lustful way. I found we had some nice conversations and several things in common, but God was helping me to control inappropriate thoughts and motives."

Tina sets a great example for guys and girls fighting lust. In the midst of real temptation, she cried out to God and received help. Then she began to honor the guy by appreciating him for who he was, not merely seeing him as an object to desire. She also added what John Piper calls a "supreme regard for God" in the way she viewed her circumstances. She began to see her behavior and interactions as a chance to glorify God, who is holy and wants her to be holy.

"Changing how you view dating and interactions with the opposite sex is quite a challenge," Tina admits. "Constant focus on God is key!" And it's the key to victory over lust.

---

1. This material was taken from John Piper's sermon "Battling the Unbelief of Lust." To order a tape of this sermon, contact: Desiring God Ministries, Bethlehem Baptist Church, 720 13th Avenue, South Minneapolis, MN 55415; 1-888-346-4700; www.DesiringGod.org.

CHAPTER TWELVE

Redeeming the Time

Making the Most of Your Singleness

CHAPTER AT A GLANCE

This chapter addresses that time in a single's life when he or she could marry, and hasn't yet met a suitable partner. Instead of worrying about when this "special someone" will arrive, we're challenged to follow the instruction of Ephesians 5:15 and "redeem the time." We may not know the next step regarding romance, but we can use today to move toward maturity and Christlikeness.

The story of Rebekah in the Old Testament illustrates how faithfully carrying out our current obligations positions us to meet God's divine appointment for our lives. We must be faithful in the relationships we have now if we want to be prepared to pursue faithfulness and growth in marriage later.

We're given five areas in which we can prepare while we're single:

1. *Practice intimacy.* In our homes and in other friendships, we should learn the art of sharing our lives with others by being open and honest.
2. *Practice seeking God with others.* To prepare for a dynamic spiritual life in marriage, we should learn to talk about and share our faith with other believers.
3. *Practice financial responsibility.* Now is the time to learn to manage money wisely. This includes saving, tithing, and keeping a budget.

4. *Practice parenthood.* We should observe how skilled parents raise their children and seek opportunities to learn from them.
5. *Practice practical life skills.* We'll greatly bless our future husband or wife if we learn how to manage and care for a home before we get married.

Finally, we're reminded that marriage is not the finish line. We prepare and develop our character so we can be as useful as possible for God no matter what He plans for our future.

KEY QUOTE

"When we focus on 'redeeming the time,' we'll not only make the most of each moment; we'll also prepare ourselves for the next season of our lives. Our faithfulness in small things today earns us the right to handle bigger responsibilities down the road."

KEY SCRIPTURE

Ephesians 5:15–16: "Be very careful, then, how you live—not as unwise but as wise, making the most of every opportunity, because the days are evil."

GOAL OF DISCUSSION

The purpose of this discussion is to consider ways we can make the most of our singleness. What responsibilities has God called us to fulfill today? How can we use this time to prepare for our future?

ICEBREAKERS

1. Do you have well-meaning family members and friends with that matchmaking gleam in their eye? What are your experiences?
2. In what ways have you "redeemed the time" in your everyday life?

GETTING SERIOUS

1. How can developing intimacy with our family members prepare us for marriage?
2. Why is it important not to view marriage as the goal or finish line? What is our ultimate reason for redeeming the time?

BEING REAL

1. Josh's dad says, "Rebekah was able to meet God's divine appointment for her life because she was faithfully carrying out her current obligations" (page 157). What does "watering camels" look like for you?
2. Are you spending more time dreaming about your future than preparing for it? What responsibilities do you need to fulfill today?
3. How can you "practice parenthood" right now?
4. What's a practical life skill you will work on developing in the next six months?

JUST FOR GUYS

How responsible are you when it comes to your finances? What changes do you need to make in your spending habits?

JUST FOR GIRLS

What's one way you can practice seeking God with others?

REFLECTION

Every January I host a conference for singles age eighteen to twenty-nine called New Attitude (you can learn more about this event at www.newattitude.org). Our first year about a thousand people came from across the country to learn more about God, worship Him, and enjoy fellowship with like-minded believers.

I had the honor of giving the conference's final message. What was I going to say? I was sobered by the responsibility. *What is the most important message I can send home with a thousand Christian singles?* I asked myself. *What does God want ringing in their ears?*

The topic I chose may have surprised some people. The title was "Passion for the Church." My message was simple. As Christians, God wants us to be passionate about His plan for the church and to demonstrate this in the way we live. We need to be committed to our local church, serving and growing in it, and building our lives around it.

I'm sure some expected a visionary message on how our conference would grow to tens of thousands of people. ("So go home and start telling your friends about next year!") But I don't believe that was God's heart for those singles. Conferences are fine, but the thing God wants to build, the institution against which He promised the gates of hell would not stand, is His church.

Chapter 12 talks about redeeming the time and making the most of our singleness. But that pursuit is never to be self-centered; it's to be God-centered—built around His plans and His kingdom. That's why redeeming the time as a single involves active service and growth in a local church. It's through the church that God wants to demonstrate to the world what His kingdom is all about.

Many people today—especially young people—have lost their vision for the church. We think of it as merely a building or a place to go for social interaction. The choices we make reveal how low a priority it is to us. We put everything before it—our education, our career, and our own comfort. But God's Word says, "The church...is not peripheral to the world; the world is peripheral to the church. The church is Christ's body, in which he speaks and acts, by which he fills everything with his presence" (Ephesians 1:23, *The Message*). The church is at the center of God's plan, not on the outskirts. And it shouldn't be on the outskirts of our lives either.

My good friend Andrew recently cut back his work hours at Starbucks so he could serve more in our church's college ministry. Andrew is also a student and his life is busy, but he realized the need to make God's priorities his priorities. He didn't want his involvement in church to be limited to attending meetings or enjoying time with friends. He wanted to be actively participating and serving.

Are you active and committed in your church? Does your pastor know of and feel your support? Are you volunteering to serve, and are you dependable when you do?

God has given us the local church for our good. What a source of comfort, encouragement, and support it can be. If you're not part of a church, please find one. Make it a priority to join a strong Bible-teaching (and living) church where you can build relationships, be challenged to grow, and most important, redeem the time by using your singleness to serve others.

CHAPTER THIRTEEN

◦◦◦

Ready for the Sack but Not for the Sacrifice

How to Have a Biblical and Realistic Vision of Marriage

CHAPTER AT A GLANCE

This chapter shows that singles often have a limited and unrealistic view of marriage, focusing on the fun and exciting aspects of marriage—such as the wedding ceremony or the pleasure of a physical relationship—but failing to think about the hard work and sacrifice marriage requires.

Next, we're shown God's purpose for marriage found in the Bible. Marriage is the first institution God created (Genesis 2:22–24); it depicts the supernatural union between Jesus and the church (Ephesians 5:31–32); it is the event God has selected to consummate all of time (Revelation 19:7); and it is to be held in honor (Hebrews 13:4).

Finally, we look at our responsibility in marriage. We see that it is a process that will refine and cleanse us from our selfishness and sin. Marriage requires guts, maturity, and character. Only when we cultivate these qualities and disciplines can we carry out our responsibilities and experience true joy and fulfillment in marriage. The chapter closes with a poem that challenges men to grasp the price of a woman's love and encourages women to keep their standards for a husband high.

KEY QUOTE

"As singles we face the important task of cultivating a balanced, biblical understanding of God's purpose and plan for marriage. Marriage is not to be, in the words of an old wedding sermon, 'enterprised lightly or wantonly to satisfy man's carnal lusts and appetites, but reverently, discreetly, advisedly, soberly and in the fear of God, duly considering the causes for which matrimony was ordained.'"

KEY SCRIPTURE

Hebrews 13:4: "Marriage should be honored by all." (Also see Genesis 2:22–24; Ephesians 5:31–32; and Revelation 19:7.)

GOAL OF DISCUSSION

We want to come away from this chapter with a biblical and realistic view of marriage. Are we really ready for the sacrifice it requires? What qualities do we need to cultivate to prepare for marriage?

ICEBREAKERS

1. Like Josh's wedding videos, movies are a glamorized version of reality. How would a glamorized version of your past week be different from what actually happened?
2. Share an example of a strong marriage that you have observed.

GETTING SERIOUS

1. How is the Bible's definition of marriage radically different from the world's?
2. What would marriages in America look like if we truly upheld and practiced the Bible's view of marriage?

BEING REAL

1. What aspect of marriage (the wedding ceremony, sex, or something else) do you find yourself concentrating on, to the exclusion of all others?
2. On a scale of one to ten, how prepared are you for the sacrifices of marriage? What do you need to do to be ready?
3. Give examples of ways you can view marriage with "reverence" and "discretion" as well as "advisedly" and "soberly" (see definitions on page 167)?
4. How can you encourage others to hold marriage in high esteem?

JUST FOR GUYS

What was your reaction to "A Woman's Question" (pages 172–3)? (Hint: If it didn't send chills up your spine, then you're not ready for marriage.) How can you earn the right to ask a woman to marry you?

JUST FOR GIRLS

Josh writes, "In our daydreams about marriage, we too often forget what a drastic course of action marriage really is" (page 172). What qualities can you cultivate now in preparation for marriage?

REFLECTION

I received an e-mail from a girl who was concerned about my decision not to kiss my future wife until we were married. She had talked to a friend who said that without some form of physical interaction before marriage, there could be damaging effects on our sex life.

I answered her by saying that the transition a couple makes between no physical contact and full consummation is important, but that it should take place after marriage, not before it. There's no rule that says newlyweds have to have sex their first night together.

The emphasis for both people (especially the guy) should be on serving the other person, not demanding gratification. Part of the beauty of two partners who have not "known" each other sexually is discovery and a mutual learning experience.

"I don't plan to be an 'expert in bed' when I get married," I wrote. And that shouldn't be anyone's goal. Our main concern as Christians should be purity before God, not being experienced lovers when we get married.

I share this story as an example of how we're often more concerned with being "ready for the sack" than we are with being "ready for the sacrifice." I wonder if the girl who wrote me has ever had an in-depth conversation about whether or not she and her friend are preparing themselves for the hard work of serving, loving, honoring, and communicating with their future husbands. We should be more concerned about developing these skills than being "good in bed."

The root cause of our preoccupation with the wrong things is an undue focus on ourselves and our own needs. The reason we so often have an immature view of marriage is because our outlook on life is self-centered. That's why the main question chapter 13 confronts is whether our view of marriage is based on selfishness or selflessness.

The possibility of marriage might be far off for you, but it's not too early to begin to change your outlook. Start developing an others-centered view of life. How can you serve your family and friends? How can you lay down your own desires to do what's best for someone else? Meditate on Christ's words in Luke 9:23–24: "If anyone would come after me, he must deny himself and take up his cross daily and follow me. For whoever wants to save his life will lose it, but whoever loses his life for me will save it." Look for ways to give your life away by serving others.

We live in a world that wants to pull us toward selfishness—to be more concerned with personal pleasure than sacrificial living. But God's Word says, "Each of you should look not only to your own interests, but also to the interests of others" (Philippians 2:4).

It's this others-centered attitude that will help us have a biblical and realistic vision of marriage. Are we merely excited about the pleasurable aspects of marriage—sexual intimacy, companionship, and security? Or are we also ready to embrace the sacrifice of marriage—serving our spouse, working to communicate, and offering forgiveness when we're wronged?

The way we live as singles is preparing us for one or the other.

CHAPTER FOURTEEN

What Matters at Fifty?

Character Qualities and Attitudes That Matter Most in a Life Partner

CHAPTER AT A GLANCE

This chapter deals with the qualities that matter most in a spouse and challenges us to get past the surface issues of looks, dress, and performance in front of others—issues that won't "matter at fifty."

We look at two criteria by which to evaluate a person and are encouraged to maintain a humble attitude of self-examination. How are we doing in these areas?

1. *Character*—which is defined by the choices and decisions a person has made and makes each day. We can evaluate a person's character by observing how he or she relates to God and whether or not the individual has a dynamic, growing, personal relationship with Him. We can also look at *the way he or she treats others,* such as authorities, parents, and members of the opposite sex. Finally, we can take note of *the way this person disciplines his or her personal life* regarding the use of time, money, and care of his or her body.
2. *Attitude*—which is how a person looks at and reacts to life. A godly attitude is expressed through willing obedience to God, humility, industriousness, as well as contentment and hopefulness.

These qualities help us know what to look for in another person and what to work on in our own lives.

KEY QUOTE

"We're too easily impressed by image; God wants us to value qualities that will last. Wisely choosing a marriage partner requires that we get back to the essentials of a person's character and attitude.... We need to concentrate not only on *finding* the right person but, more important, on *becoming* the right person."

KEY SCRIPTURE

1 Samuel 16:7: "Man looks at the outward appearance, but the LORD looks at the heart." (Also see Psalm 119:60; Proverbs 31:17, 30; 2 Corinthians 6:14; and Philippians 2:3.)

GOAL OF DISCUSSION

The goal of this chapter is to answer this question: "What qualities should we look for in a spouse?" Are we more impressed by image and physical beauty than biblical qualities that will last? More important, are we becoming the right kind of people ourselves?

ICEBREAKERS

1. Let's try this humorous twist on Josh's "What matters at fifty?" game (pages 175–6): What do you think *you* will look like when you're fifty?
2. What's an unimportant, innocent quality (i.e., likes country music, is taller or shorter than you) that you would like in a spouse?

GETTING SERIOUS

1. Why is it most important to choose a spouse who loves Jesus more than anything else?
2. In what specific ways is an attitude of industriousness vital to a successful marriage?

BEING REAL

1. Before reading this chapter, what qualities were at the top of your list for a potential spouse? How have your desires changed?
2. If we interviewed your parents today, how would they describe the way you relate to them? What areas do you need to improve in as a son or daughter that will prepare you to be a better husband or wife?

3. Think about the way you use time, handle money, and care for your body. What's one area where you most need to grow in personal discipline?
4. Remember the story of Mrs. E. V. Hill (pages 183–4)? What's a difficult situation in your life in which you can choose to focus on the good like she did?

JUST FOR GUYS

What do your companions—those you enjoy being with most—reveal about your character? What friendships can you cultivate that would encourage your walk with the Lord?

JUST FOR GIRLS

Where do you stand on the friendly-flirtatious scale? How do you need to change your attitudes and actions toward members of the opposite sex?

REFLECTION

What matters at fifty? At the end of this year, I'll be twenty-five years old—halfway there. What does it mean to be a grown-up? As I approach this symbolic birthday, I realize my ideas about adulthood have been mixed up.

Even though a big part of growing up is being able to stand on your own feet, a focus on achieving independence and self-sufficiency can have the damaging effect of crowding out gratitude. We often see the journey to adulthood as a process of shedding dependence on our parents. But I'm beginning to realize that true maturity isn't measured in the dependence we can throw off, but in the responsibility we can take on. We mistakenly believe that maturity is in not needing others, when in fact maturity is responding as servants to those who need us.

How many of us make the same mistake the nine ungrateful lepers of Jesus' day made (see Luke 17:12–18)? In our excitement about our own lives and expanding horizons, we rush on our way without a thought to go back and thank those who made these opportunities possible. I am convinced that most of the conflicts I see my peers facing with their parents would be solved if they looked through eyes of gratitude instead of a self-centeredness that asks, "Why do I need them anymore?"

I don't want this to be my attitude. I hope it isn't yours. Now is the time in our lives when we can begin to express our gratefulness to our dad and mom and in small ways attempt the impossible task of paying them back for all they've done for us.

This isn't to say all parents are without fault. Yours may not be Christians or may not show you love. Honoring and showing our gratefulness to our parents, however, reveals that we trust and believe in God's providence. He gave us our parents, and He calls us to honor them. He's also promised to bless those who do. In Ephesians 6:2–3, Paul exhorts the believers to "'Honor your father and mother'—which is the first commandment with a promise—'that it may go well with you and that you may enjoy long life on the earth.'"

The ways *you* can honor your dad and mom will be different than those of other people. A spirit of gratitude shows itself in big and small ways. Whether your parents need a special gift and a hug, or the more practical expression of a chore cheerfully completed, be on the lookout for opportunities.

Above all, enjoy your parents. Appreciate them in spite of their imperfections. Don't let another day go by that you don't make an investment into the life that has given so much to you. I have a feeling that someday you and I will want our kids to do the same.

❦

Principled Romance

Principles That Can Guide
You from Friendship to Matrimony

CHAPTER AT A GLANCE

This chapter outlines a new pattern for relationships that can help us avoid the problems with typical dating. Although the Bible doesn't provide a one-size-fits-all program for moving from friendship to marriage, we can honor God when we follow godly patterns and principles for romance.

The stages of this pattern are: casual friendship, deeper friendship, courtship, and engagement. Within this pattern we're given some important principles that can guide us:

1. *Remember your relational responsibilities.* When you feel attracted to someone, remember that although you are not the "center of the universe," your actions affect your relationship with the person you're interested in, your relationship with your family and friends, and your relationship with God.
2. *Seek a deeper friendship first.* Focus on developing a closer friendship with a potential partner before introducing romance. Don't change your routine; instead look for opportunities to bring that person into your real life. Wait to verbally express your feelings.
3. *Watch, wait, and pray.* If you feel inclined to deepen a relationship with a guy or girl, it's always wise to take extra time to get to know the person better as a friend and to seek God's guidance. Seek the counsel of a few older, trusted Christians (ideally, this should

include your parents). Ask them to pray for you, and invite them to keep you accountable about the relationship.

4. *Define the relationship's purpose: pursuing marriage.* It's the guy's responsibility to clearly state his intentions and provide leadership and direction for the relationship.

5. *Honor her parents.* The man should show respect by asking the girl's parents for permission to pursue marriage with their daughter and inviting their perspective.

6. *Test and build the relationship in real-life settings.* This is the time for the young man to win the girl's heart and for the two of them to test the wisdom of their potential marriage. This period need last only as long as it takes for both to feel confident about getting married.

7. *Reserve passion for marriage.* Protect each other by refusing to physically express your love until the proper time.

Principled romance is purposeful in its pursuit of marriage, protected in its avoidance of sexual temptation, and accountable to parents or other Christians.

KEY QUOTE

"The various ways in which God brings men and women together, like the unique designs of snowflakes, are never quite the same. But just as a one-of-a-kind snowflake can only form at a specific temperature and precipitation, a God-honoring romance can only form when we follow godly patterns and principles."

KEY SCRIPTURE

Galatians 5:22: "But the fruit of the Spirit is love, joy, peace, patience, kindness, goodness, faithfulness, gentleness and self-control." (Also see Proverbs 29:20; Song of Songs 8:4; and Ephesians 5:23–25.)

GOAL OF DISCUSSION

Our objective for this chapter is to discuss how to practically move from friendship to marriage in a way that glorifies God. What are helpful questions to ask and principles to follow as we pursue a deeper relationship?

ICEBREAKERS

1. What kinds of activities can a guy and girl do together to develop a more-than-casual friendship?

2. Girls, you can help the guys out by answering this one: What things should be left unsaid by guys until you're both ready to pursue a commitment?

GETTING SERIOUS

1. If now is not God's timing for you to pursue a relationship, how did this chapter give you something to look forward to?
2. How can romance actually hinder first developing a friendship with someone?

BEING REAL

1. Are you pursuing a relationship in which you have one or more "red lights"? What are they, and how might you need to "stop"?
2. Who do you need to get guidance and oversight from before pursuing a relationship? Have you gone to them? Why or why not?
3. Which of the principles shared in this chapter do you think you'd have the most trouble living by? Why do you think it would be difficult?
4. If you aren't in a relationship right now, how can you serve and support your friends who are?

JUST FOR GUYS

In what specific ways can you lead and provide direction for a relationship?

JUST FOR GIRLS

Are you being completely honest with a guy who is pursuing you? How should you be responding?

REFLECTION

Principled romance is not for the faint of heart—it's for those willing to live courageously.

Chapter 15 gives us a glimpse of what it looks like to apply the principles of *I Kissed Dating Goodbye* to an unfolding relationship. It shows how we can pursue romance in a way that models Christ's love, is pointed in the direction of purity, and constantly looks to Him for guidance.

This journey requires faith. A formula would be easy. A twelve-step program of courtship that told us what to do and when to do it wouldn't require self-control, patience, endurance, and childlike trust in God. That's why God doesn't give us a formula. Instead He gives us fundamental truths—principles—in His Word on which to build our lives. Then He asks us to live courageously.

What does courage have to do with love? I believe it's the ingredient missing from relationships today. There's no need for courage in dating. You can play as long as you like and quit anytime you wish. There's no need for careful, quiet observation of a person's character. You don't have to search out the counsel of the wise. You can skip serious thought or passionate petitioning of God. Today's dating relationships negate the need for such bothersome toil. People date another person till they're practically married and enjoy all the emotional, social, and even sexual benefits of marriage without ever having to make the scary decision of committing to that person for the rest of their life.

And if they do decide to tie the knot, our culture has watered down marriage to make it more palatable for the cowardly. Divorce continues dating's easy-out policy. Today the journey of marriage comes complete with exit ramps. Both partners know they can get off whenever the road gets too bumpy or uncomfortable. But in choosing this route, they miss out on the joy and safety of commitment-based love.

I hope you won't make this mistake. I pray you'll have the courage to wait until you're ready for commitment to pursue a relationship. I pray you'll have the courage to fight your own sinful desires and practice purity. I also pray you'll have the courage to admit that you don't know it all and be humble enough to invite the wisdom and counsel of others. And at the right time, in a world that's afraid of commitment, I pray you'll have the courage to promise yourself to another until death parts you.

Only the courageous follow God's path. And only those who walk in His path experience the joy and peace He offers.

CHAPTER SIXTEEN

Someday I'll Have a Story to Tell

Writing a Love Story You'll Feel Proud to Tell

CHAPTER AT A GLANCE

In this chapter, Josh "time travels" in his imagination to watch his parents' love story unfold. As he recounts the unique events of their lives, he is reminded that someday he'll tell his children the story he is writing with his life today.

KEY QUOTE

"Someday I'll have a story to tell. So will you. How will you respond when one day you look back on your love story? Will it bring tears of joy or tears of remorse? Will it remind you of God's goodness or your lack of faith in that goodness? Will it be a story of purity, faith, and selfless love? Or will it be a story of impatience, selfishness, and compromise? It's your choice."

KEY SCRIPTURE

Psalm 100:5: "For the LORD is good and his love endures forever; his faithfulness continues through all generations."

GOAL OF DISCUSSION

In this final discussion, we want to stop and examine what kind of story we are writing with our lives. Is it a story we'll be proud to tell ten, twenty, fifty years from now?

ICEBREAKERS

1. Do you have a favorite family story that you love hearing over and over again?
2. What's some advice you have received from someone in a different season of life? How helpful (or unhelpful) has it been?

GETTING SERIOUS

1. How can the story of Josh's parents (pages 203–7) be an encouragement and example for us to follow?
2. In the midst of the messiness, confusion, and questions in life, what can give us hope as we pursue God's will for our lives?

BEING REAL

1. Fast-forward twenty years. How do you think you'll feel when you look back on this time in your life?
2. What effect does it have on you to think of your kids coming back in time and watching you right now?
3. Describe what changes have taken place in your life as a result of reading I Kissed Dating Goodbye. How would your story be different if you hadn't read it?
4. Would you recommend I Kissed Dating Goodbye to someone else? What would you say?

JUST FOR GUYS

What are you experiencing now that you'll want to remember so you can help someone else?

JUST FOR GIRLS

What questions about your future do you need to leave in God's hands?

REFLECTION

"But how did they get together?" That's the question many readers asked after reading the abridged version of my parents' love story told in chapter 16. Many scolded me for leaving them hanging with the line "the rest is history." To satisfy their curiosity, I'll use this space to finish the story.

As you may recall, my mom had asked God to tell my dad not to call her. When he didn't call, her interest began to grow. He either liked someone else or maybe, just maybe, he really did hear God's voice. That possibility intrigued her.

Nothing happened between them for two months. They saw each other at church functions and continued to observe each other from a distance. Then came the fateful Sunday morning announcement: Volunteers were needed to move books for the church's new library. Of course this didn't seem fateful at the time it was announced, but it became so when my mom and dad were the only two volunteers to show up.

They talked and laughed as they loaded and carried box after box of books. As a dancer who loved the arts, my mom was impressed by my dad's exposure to poetry and music. Unlike many of the boys from the Midwest she'd met, he knew the difference between a ballet dancer and a belly dancer. They found they had many common interests and experiences. Both had been to California and parts of Colorado, and both took their new faith very seriously. A friendship was born.

In the weeks that followed, the frequent number of church services they attended helped them get to know each other even better. My mom had been able to watch my dad since he had come back to the church. It was evident that God was at work in his life. He was growing and changing. Dad saw a zeal in my mom and willingness to renounce everything for the Lord. He had seen her share her faith with her family and have almost all of them, including her Buddhist grandmother, put their faith in Christ.

Surprisingly, they didn't really date each other. That was partly because there wasn't much to do in Dayton and partly because my dad was broke. Instead they would have dinner at their parents' and then go witnessing together at the mall and area parks. It was in these times of living out their faith side by side that they fell in love.

Besides all these spiritual reasons, they were just plain smitten with each other. Dad was tan and handsome—people said he looked like Olympic swimmer Mark Spitz. And in my dad's eyes, my mother was "an oriental princess" that he couldn't believe liked him.

They were married February 16, 1974. Dad says he was sure the day would come when Mom would wake up and say, "Who is this guy? What am I doing with you?" But it hasn't happened. This year they celebrated their twenty-fifth anniversary. At the anniversary party during a time when friends and family honored them, I read chapter 16 to recount God's goodness in bringing them together. And I thanked them for writing a love story with their lives that brings glory to God and that I can be so proud to tell.

I Kissed Dating Goodbye
Video Series

Study Questions

These questions are designed to be used after watching the I Kissed Dating Goodbye Video Series (previously titled the Searching for True Love video series). They can be used to guide discussion about what you have learned from the videos. We encourage you to use these videos in conjunction with the book and study guide.

VIDEO 1: LOVE

We're all searching for true love. In this video, Josh tells us where to find it.

1. What was your reaction to the responses from the people interviewed on the streets of New York? Did any particular answer stand out? What did you think of their ideas about "true love"?
2. How can humankind's search for true love be met?
3. Josh outlines three things the Bible says about true love:

   • True love lays down its life for others (John 15:13).
   • True love is sincere (Romans 12:9).
   • True love is revealed in Jesus' dying for us on the cross (John 3:16).

   How do these definitions of true love line up with your own?
   How might you apply the Bible's definitions of true love in your life today?

4. How did the dramatization of Josh's dream, "The Room," affect you?
5. Are you ready to end your search for true love by approaching the cross?

VIDEO 2: PURITY

Purity seems to be a foreign concept to many people. In this video, Josh tells us why purity still matters.

1. Do your actions reflect purity and cause others to look toward Christ? How might you need to change some of your actions?
2. Let's talk about the street interviews: Were you surprised at how difficult it was for people to define purity? Why do you think that is?
3. If you were asked, how would *you* define purity?
4. Is purity simply out of fashion today? Is there any point in even trying?
5. Josh says that purity is a direction you choose, a pursuit of righteousness. He said that a lifestyle of purity:

   • respects the beauty and sacredness of God's plan for sex in marriage (Hebrews 13:4).
   • must be motivated by awareness of God's holiness and hatred of sin (1 Peter 1:15).
   • makes the purity of others a priority (Hebrews 10:24).

   Do these definitions fit with your beliefs about purity?

6. What's your motivation for living a life of purity?
7. Have you made mistakes in the past related to your purity? God is ready to forgive you and welcome you into a *new* lifestyle of purity. Are you ready to take that step?

VIDEO 3: TRUST

Trusting God with our love life is hard, isn't it? Josh reminds us why trusting God's timing for our love life is always the best way to go.

1. Do you believe that God knows what's best for your love life? If you do, have you been open about your trust in Him?
2. Could you relate to the people being interviewed about what it's like to be single? Have you experienced that loneliness? How has God made Himself sufficient for you during those times?

3. Josh shares three characteristics of people who trust God with their love life. They:

   - redeem the time (Ephesians 5:15–16).
   - view any season in life (including a season of singleness) as a gift from God (Philippians 4:11–13).
   - make *Him* their source of hope and their refuge (Psalm 91:2).

   Are these characteristics evident in your life?

4. How can you guard against an attitude of impatience in relation to your love life?
5. What can you do with your time of singleness? Have you asked God what His mission is for you during this time?
6. During times of loneliness, God wants you to draw near to Him. How can you learn to turn to God's open arms and rely completely on Him?

The publisher and author would love to hear your comments about this book. *Please contact us at:* www.multnomah.net/ikdg

Thanks...

To Apple Computers for the PowerBook G3.

To all the people who read *I Kissed Dating Goodbye* and were radical enough to start living it. And to all the readers who asked us, and then waited patiently, for a study guide.

To all the readers who wrote and shared from their own lives. Your stories added so much to this project.

To Nicole Whitacre, who worked so hard to make the questions interesting, challenging, and thought-provoking.

To Jennifer Gott, who heroically edited this new version of the study guide and wrote the video discussion questions. Thank you!

To C. J. and Carolyn Mahaney. On behalf of Shannon and Nicole, I want to express our love and respect. The content in the book is the direct result of your investment in all three of our lives.

To my parents, Gregg and Sono, for cheering me on and praying for me from two thousand miles away.

To my bride, Shannon. We finished our first project together! I love you so much.

To my Lord and Savior, Jesus. Isaiah 26:12 will speak for me: "LORD, you establish peace for us; all that we have accomplished you have done for us."

—*Joshua Harris*

About the Authors

This study guide was a team effort of the following people:

Nicole Whitacre wrote the discussion questions. She and her husband, Steve, just had their first child, Jack. She's currently using her writing gifts to assist her mom, Carolyn Mahaney, with the writing of Carolyn's second book, which addresses mothers and daughters.

Shannon Harris wrote the chapter summaries. She's a homemaker who invests her life in the care of her two children, Emma and Joshua Quinn. She's also a gifted singer who uses her talent on her church's worship team as well as on worship recordings from Sovereign Grace Ministries.

Joshua Harris edited the study guide and wrote the reflections for each chapter. His second book, *Boy Meets Girl: Say Hello to Courtship,* is the follow-up to *I Kissed Dating Goodbye*. It focuses on the season of courtship in romance and how couples can pursue God-honoring relationships. His third book, *Not Even a Hint: Guarding Your Heart Against Lust,* was released September 2003. Josh serves as pastor at Covenant Life Church in Gaithersburg, Maryland.

To contact Josh regarding speaking and other matters, you can reach him at the following address. Although he can't reply personally to every letter, he loves mail and welcomes your feedback on this book. Write:

Joshua Harris
P.O. Box 249
Gaithersburg, MD 20884-0249
www.joshharris.com

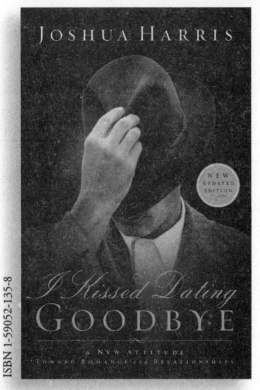

LUST TELLS YOU LIES.
THE TRUTH SETS YOU FREE.

I wrote this book for both men and women. Why? Because lust isn't a male problem. It's a human problem. Lust ruins our relationships, robs us of spiritual passion, and leaves us feeling hollow...

But the truth is that you and I don't have to stay on that treadmill of guilt and shame. God calls us to a high standard—not even a hint of sexual impurity. And He gives us everything we need to make it a reality.

If you're ready for a practical, grace-centered plan for defeating lust and celebrating purity, I hope you'll join me on a most promising journey.

—Joshua Harris

ISBN 1-59052-147-1

BOY MEETS GIRL. NOW WHAT?

I Kissed Dating Goodbye shocked the publishing world in 1995 with its metoric rise to the top of bestseller lists. Teens wanted more than dating "rules"—they wanted an intentional, God-pleasing game plan. In this dynamic sequel, newlyweds Joshua and Shannon Harris deliver an inspiring and practical illustration of how this healthy, joyous alternative to recreational dating—biblical courtship—worked for them.

Boy Meets Girl helps readers understand how to go about pursuing the possibility of marriage with someone they may be serious about. It's the natural follow-up to the author's blockbuster book on teen dating!

ISBN 1-57673-709-8

I KISSED DATING GOODBYE
VIDEO SERIES

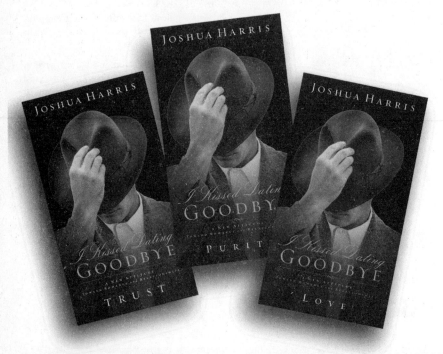

The I Kissed Dating Goodbye video series by Joshua Harris builds on his highly popular conference series and bestselling book to give young adults God's direction as they seek a lifetime love. Available in a three-pack or separately, the videos explore love, purity, and trust from the Bible's perspective. Fast-paced and engaging, each video features real-life stories, on-the-street interviews, and dynamic messages from Josh. Perfect for small groups or Sunday school classes. Forty-five minutes each.

I Kissed Dating Goodbye Video-Part 1: Love   ISBN 1-59052-212-5

I Kissed Dating Goodbye Video-Part 1: Purity   ISBN 1-59052-213-3

I Kissed Dating Goodbye Video-Part 1: Trust   ISBN 1-59052-214-1

Three-video series   ISBN 1-59052-180-3